INCREDIBLE **TRUE** ADVENTURES

THE SINKING OF THE *TITANIC*
AND OTHER SHIPWRECKS

ANITA GANERI & DAVID WEST

rosen publishing's
rosen
central

New York

Published in 2012 by The Rosen Publishing Group, Inc.
29 East 21st Street, New York, NY 10010

Designed and produced by
David West Books

Designer: Gary Jeffrey
Editor: Katharine Pethick
Illustrator: David West

Picture credits:
2t, 29tl, NOAA Ocean Explorer; 8m, Christine Matthews; 9mr, Peter
Isotalo; 11m, 13main, 13mr, 29tr, 41bl, NOAA; 13tr, xornalcerto; 13bl,
13tl, Institute for Exploration/Univer (NOAA); 16t, 16bl, Naval
Historical Center; 16bl, U.S. Navy Photo; 17t dbking; 20bl, USCG; 25br,
Museum of Cultural History, University of Oslo, Norway; 28main, 40br,
Library of Congress; 29bl, PH1 (A W/NAC) Martin Maddock (NOAA);
29ml, NOAA Ocean Explorer (boot_600); 29m, 29br, PH1 Chadwick
Vann (NOAA); 33tr, Georges Jansoone; 33bl, 33bm, 33br, Martin
Bahmann; 32ml, Dale McDonald Collection; State Library and Archives
of Florida; 37mmr, Augi Garcia; 36–37, Elkman; 40tr, x-ray delta one;
40bl, Library of Congress, Prints and Photographs Collections; 41tr, US
Army; 41mrb, Ben Sutherland;

Library of Congress Cataloging-in-Publication Data

Ganeri, Anita, 1961-
The sinking of the Titanic and other shipwrecks / Anita Ganeri, David
West.
p. cm. -- (Incredible true stories)
Includes bibliographical references and index.
ISBN 978-1-4488-6659-5 (library binding) -- ISBN 978-1-4488-6663-2
(pbk.) -- ISBN 978-1-4488-6671-7 (6-pack)
1. Titanic (Steamship)--Juvenile literature. 2. Shipwrecks--North
Atlantic Ocean--Juvenile literature. I. West, David. II. Title.
G530.T6G353 2012
910.9163'1--dc23
2011031168

Printed in China

CPSIA Compliance Information Batch #DWW12YA:
For further information contact Rosen Publishing, New York, New York, at 1-800-237-9932.

CONTENTS

INTRODUCTION

The ocean floor is littered with the wrecks of ships lost or destroyed at sea. Some ran aground on rocks or coral reefs; others ran into bad weather or sank in battle. Many have been rediscovered by divers using the latest in underwater technology. Their stories make fascinating reading, as they offer up their secrets from the deep.

An underwater archaeologist explores a weed-encrusted wreck site.

The remains of an ocean liner lying wrecked on a distant shore.

FIND OUT MORE

SINKING OF THE MARY ROSE

"I'm afraid she's lost sire, lost!"

As the courtier whispered these words into the king's ear, a gasp went up from the crowd. Before their horrified eyes, the *Mary Rose*, the king's flagship, began to roll over and sink.

It was July 19, 1545. England was at war with France, and the *Mary Rose* was leading the English fleet out to fight the French in the English Channel. From nearby Plymouth, King Henry VIII watched with pride as the *Mary Rose* fired a broadside at the enemy ships and then swung around so that the guns on its other side could fire. Then disaster struck.

As the wind picked up, the ship tipped sharply to one side, and water rushed in through its open gun ports.

In an instant, in front of their very eyes, the once-proud *Mary Rose* rolled over and started to sink. The cries of the terrified crew carried across the water to the crowd. But there was little chance of escape.

FIND OUT MORE

FINDING THE WRECK

Of the 700 men on board, fewer than 40 survived. Almost immediately, the king launched a rescue mission, but the ship was too heavy to lift. More than 400 years later, a team of divers led by Alexander McKee rediscovered the wreck's whereabouts.

The Mary Rose as shown on a 1546 inventory of English ships

RAISING THE SHIP

In October 1982, after centuries under water, the fragile ship's hull was supported by a steel frame, lifted onto a steel cradle lined with airbags, and raised from the water. The ship is now housed in a dry dock in Portsmouth Historic Dockyard in England.

The Mary Rose *in dry dock two years after it was lifted*

King Henry VIII's favorite warship, the Mary Rose, *gives a fascinating glimpse of Tudor life. A specially built museum (left) will soon display the ship, together with many of the artifacts found with it.*

Bronze cannon

WRECK OF THE VASA

Another famous royal warship, the *Vasa*, sank in Stockholm harbor in August 1628 within hours of being launched. The ship was caught in a squall and capsized, with few survivors. In 1956, amateur marine archaeologist Anders Franzen discovered the wreck lying 115 feet (35 meters) down in the seabed mud. It was raised in 1961.

The Vasa had a top-heavy design with not enough keel or ballast stones.

The Vasa on display in its museum in Stockholm, Sweden

A scale model of the Vasa (above), shows how its brightly painted stern once looked.

Antiship cannon

Many 17th-century artifacts were rescued with the Vasa, including weapons and personal items.

Chain shot

Bar shot

A backgammon game

DISCOVERY OF THE TITANIC

"The sheer size of her is awesome!"

Through the portholes of their submersible, *Alvin*, Robert Ballard and his colleagues peered in amazement at the enormous, ghostly, gray shape. The sight sent shivers down their spines. Right in front of them rose the massive steel hull of RMS *Titanic*, the largest passenger liner of its day and a symbol of disaster for the 20th century. For Ballard, it was a dream come true. A year after first locating the wreck almost 2.5 miles (4 kilometers) down on the seabed of the North Atlantic Ocean, he was now back for a closer look.

More surprises lay in store. On his second dive, Ballard could clearly see the rust-covered bow with the huge anchors still in place. The following day, *Alvin* landed next to the Grand Staircase—a somber reminder of the ship's grandeur. Using Jason Junior, a robotic camera, Ballard spotted a huge chandelier and peeked inside some of the first-class cabins. Exploring the *Titanic* was like wandering through a ghost town.

It had once been a very different story. Nicknamed the Millionaires' Special, the *Titanic* was built of the finest steel and fitted out in the grandest style, with a theater, swimming pool, squash court, and Turkish bath among its many attractions. On April 14, 1912, the ship was four days into its maiden voyage from Southampton to New York. Throughout the day, other ships in the area sent warnings of icebergs drifting further south than usual for the time of year. On board the *Titanic*, the warnings were ignored.

Then, at 11:40 p.m., one of the lookouts spotted a gigantic iceberg dead ahead. Immediately the order was given to swing the ship to one side, but it was too late. The iceberg gashed a hole in *Titanic*'s side, and water began pouring in. A few minutes later, it came to a halt. Could it be that the ship labeled "practically unsinkable" was sinking fast?

FIND OUT MORE

Titanic's first-class lounge (below). No expense was spared in fitting out the opulent vessel.

The *Titanic* was divided into watertight compartments. It could still float if the first four were flooded, but water was pouring into five. At 2:20 a.m., the doomed ship turned on one end and sank. Out of 2,208 people, only 712 survived.

The Titanic leaves Southampton, UK, in April 1912.

An artist's impression of the sinking

Survivors of the disaster

TITANIC FINDS

Thousands of artifacts surround the wreck, many of them perfectly preserved. They include parts of the ship, furniture, bathtubs, cups and saucers, wine bottles, chamber pots, suitcases, and even children's toys. Thousands more artifacts have been removed and put on display in museums.

Among the artifacts scattered around the wreck are many personal items, such as these leather boots.

A top hat from the wreck

Captain Smith's cabin washroom remains (below).

Silverware raised from the Titanic *(left)*

After almost a century on the seabed, the whole ship is encrusted in long strands of reddish-brown rust. By 2050, it will be gone forever.

HUNT FOR THE BISMARCK

"Stay on target! Torpedo away!"

With these words, the crew of the tiny Swordfish bomber launched another torpedo. Below, in the near darkness, lay its target—the German Navy's mighty *Bismarck*—the biggest warship afloat.

At dusk on May 26, 1941, the Swordfish, along with its squadron, scrambled from the aircraft carrier *Ark Royal*. Hampered by atrocious weather, this was to be its final attack. The crew watched nervously as a huge column of smoke rose from the *Bismarck*'s side. The torpedo—a shot in a million—had struck home! The ship began turning helplessly in a huge circle; the strike had disabled its steering gear.

Accompanied by the *Prinz Eugen*, the *Bismarck's* mission was to attack cargo ships in the North Atlantic Ocean ferrying supplies between the United States and Britain. Meanwhile, under orders to "sink the *Bismarck*," the British Navy was determined to hunt the ship down. A fleet of warships and heavy cruisers, among them HMS *Hood*, flagship of the British fleet, had been dispatched. Then disaster struck. In an exchange of fire, the *Hood* had been directly hit by a shell from the *Bismarck*, exploded with a gigantic bang, and sank. But the *Bismarck* was not safe yet.

Having already been badly hit, the ship was heading toward the safe water of a French harbor, when the Swordfish torpedo struck.

The next day, the British fleet closed in and opened fire. Despite the pounding, the ship remained afloat for almost three hours, still flying its flag. Then, finally, at 10:38 a.m. on May 27, the mighty *Bismarck* sank. Of the crew of 2,065, only 115 survived. But was that the end of the story?

FIND OUT MORE

WAR WRECKS

For almost five decades, the *Bismarck* lay on the seabed, about 405 miles (650 kilometers) west of France. It was rediscovered in June 1989 by Robert Ballard, who had also found the *Titanic*.

Bismarck in action

BISMARCK'S SECRET

On further investigation of the *Bismarck's* hull, Ballard found evidence that the ship had been deliberately scuttled by its crew to speed up its sinking. This may have been to protect sensitive technical equipment on board.

The Bismarck lies more than half a mile (1 km) deeper than the Titanic. It was filmed using Mir (right), a Russian Deep Submergence Vehicle.

Survivors from the Bismarck were pulled aboard HMS Dorsetshire.

USS Susan B. Anthony lies at the bottom of the English Channel, as this sonar image shows.

Not all war wrecks end in tragedy. The largest rescue of people without loss of life, all 2,689 aboard, happened on the USS Susan B. Anthony. The transport ship struck a mine in 1944.

FATE OF THE *MAINE*

The USS *Maine* was an American battleship launched in 1889. On the night of February 15, 1898, while in Havana Harbor, Cuba, an explosion blew the ship apart. The cause of the explosion remains a mystery.

USS Maine, *1898*

The Maine *being salvaged in 1911*

SUNKEN MEMORIALS

Ships sunk during wartime are often considered to be war graves, meaning there are restrictions on their exploration and marine salvage. Some sites have also been preserved as memorials to sailors who died in battle.

The wreck of the USS Arizona *was not salvaged and continues to lie on the seabed at Pearl Harbor as a memorial to those who perished on December 7, 1941.*

The cataclysmic and dramatic sinking of the USS Arizona *caused the loss of 1,177 lives.*

The Arizona *as it once was. East River, New York City, 1916*

WRECK OF THE WHYDAH

"It's gold! Pirates' gold!"

The diver could not believe his eyes as he gazed at the coin in his hand, and there was more to come. He and his fellow divers unearthed thousands of gold and silver coins, as well as pistols, anchors, and other pieces of treasure—pirate treasure. It was 1984.

The divers were led by underwater explorer Barry Clifford. Relying on an 18th-century map, Clifford had located the wreck of the *Whydah*, the flagship of infamous pirate "Black Sam" Bellamy. It had sunk in a storm off Cape Cod, Massachusetts, on April 26, 1717, taking most of its crew and treasure down with it.

Bellamy's pirate spree began in the Caribbean, raiding any ships that crossed his path. It took a three-day chase to capture the *Whydah*, but it was worth the wait. The ship was sailing from Jamaica to England with a dazzling cargo of sugar, gold, silver, and ivory. Realizing that resistance was useless, the captain surrendered and escaped with his life.

Next, Bellamy headed northward along the eastern coast of America, intent on continuing his trail of plunder. Then, on April 26, disaster struck. As black clouds rolled in from the horizon, a fierce storm began to blow up. Sailing dangerously close to the coast, the *Whydah* was heading straight into it.

FIND OUT MORE

PIRATE LIFE

The *Whydah* was driven ashore at Cape Cod and quickly broke apart. Only two of its 180-man crew survived. Shipwreck was just one of the mishaps a professional pirate might face.

PIRATE SHIPS

The *Whydah* was a three-masted galley, but typical pirate ships included schooners, brigantines, and sloops. They were altered to carry more crew and cannon than normal so that they could easily overcome their victims.

Blackbeard was one of the most feared pirates of all. As well as being heavily armed, he grew a long, tangled beard to make himself look even more terrifying.

Pirate ships, like this schooner (above), were given fearsome-sounding names, like Sudden Death and Night Rambler.

"Pieces of eight," or Spanish silver dollars, were made in the Americas and transported back to Spain— easy plunder for pirates.

Port Royal, Jamaica

Notorious English pirate "Calico Jack" Rackham (right) popularized the Jolly Roger flag.

PIRATES OF THE CARIBBEAN

For pirates like Black Sam Bellamy, the Caribbean was a rich hunting ground. Islands like Jamaica became havens for pirates because they were well-placed for attacking Spanish treasure ships carrying treasure from Mexico and South America to Europe.

Pistols, blunderbusses, cutlasses, and axes were all part of a pirate's weaponry.

Women could be pirates, too. Calico Jack's girlfriend, Anne Bonny (above), joined his crew dressed as a man.

PIRATE DEATHS

If a pirate was captured, he was put on trial and then executed by hanging. This usually took place dockside or onboard a ship and attracted large crowds of onlookers.

A captured pirate's body was coated in tar and hung in an iron cage as a warning.

ATTACK OF THE FIRESHIPS

"Flee, flee for your lives—the fireships are coming!"

As the horrified lookout shouted out his warning, he knew it was already too late. Staring out to sea, he could see that the tiny pinpricks of light were approaching the harbor—fast.

With the wind blowing them toward the shore, the town's fate would soon be sealed. For the specks of light were burning ships that were filled with hay or brushwood and then set on fire. They were sent to destroy the town of Hedeby.

It was just before dawn in the year 1050. The people of Hedeby, the most important trading center in Viking Denmark, were waking up. Hedeby was a busy place, its houses close together along streets that led down to the sea. It was protected on three sides by earthworks, leaving the harbor the only open approach. Its inhabitants had been feeling safe, until now.

As the lookout's warning rang out, all eyes turned toward the harbor where the fireships were bearing down. These were Norwegian ships sent by King Harald Hardrada to score a victory over the Danish king. As the ships entered the harbor, they set light first to the other boats. Then the flames spread to the town's wooden buildings. Hedeby was doomed. By the evening, the town had burned to the ground, despite desperate efforts to save it. After Harald Hardrada's devastating attack, Hedeby was attacked and destroyed again in 1066. Its people abandoned their homes and moved across the water to the town of Schleswig. Hedeby lay forgotten, and rising sea levels submerged it under the water. Then, almost 900 years later, divers made an exciting discovery—the remains of a Viking longship in the harbor. Could this have been one of Harald's fireships? All the signs pointed to it.

FIND OUT MORE

VIKING SHIP FINDS

The wreck of the Hedeby longship was excavated in 1979 when a cofferdam was built around it and the water drained out. Archaeologists saw that the timbers were heavily charred, evidence that the ship had been set on fire in the attack on Hedeby.

Skuldelev 3

SCUTTLED IN SKULDELEV

In 1962, five Viking ships were excavated at Skuldelev in Denmark. They included three cargo ships and two warships. They were deliberately sunk around 1070 to block Roskilde Fjord and protect the town of Roskilde from enemy attacks by sea.

A preserved first-century longboat shows the sturdy overlapping, or "clinker," hull construction found on Viking vessels.

In 1893, a replica of a Viking ship (above) sailed across the Atlantic from Norway for display at the Chicago World's Fair.

Skuldelev 2, the largest longship ever found, was built in Dublin, Ireland. It could carry 80 raiders.

Burial Ships

When a Viking king or chief died, his body and grave goods were put on a ship that was then buried or burned. In 1880, an extraordinary Viking burial ship was discovered at Gokstad in Norway.

This model shows how the Gokstad ship once looked.

The Gokstad ship (left) was surrounded by blue clay, which kept it almost perfectly preserved.

The carved stern of the Oseberg burial ship (right), now at the Viking Museum in Olso, Norway.

Wooden carvings of animals have been found on some ships, giving them the name "dragon ships."

The Oseberg ship (right)

Many precious Viking artifacts, including weapons and armor, have been found in ship burial mounds.

LOSS OF THE MONITOR

"The boiler room's flooded—it's every man for himself!"

As he spoke, Captain John Bankhead knew his ship was doomed. For hours, the USS *Monitor* had been lashed by heavy seas and, at times, completely submerged. Now the water had reached the boiler room and extinguished the fires that produced steam to power the engine and pumps. Despite the crew's valiant attempts to keep the water at bay, the *Monitor* was sinking—fast.

Under tow by the USS *Rhode Island*, the *Monitor* was approaching Cape Hatteras on the coast of North Carolina and the area known as the Graveyard of the Atlantic. It had been ordered north to Beaufort from its base in Hampton Roads. The *Monitor* had already made history as the first ironclad warship in the US Navy. But, though well suited to river combat, its new and revolutionary design made the ship highly unstable in rough seas.

Realizing that everything possible had been done to save the boat, Bankhead gave the order to abandon ship and get into the two approaching rescue boats. Several men remained behind, rooted to the spot in fear. Others were washed overboard by the waves. After unloading the men onto the *Rhode Island*, the boats returned to the *Monitor*, only to find they had arrived too late.

Just after midnight on December 31, 1862, the shell-shocked survivors aboard the *Rhode Island* watched in horror as the *Monitor*'s lights went out, and it sank beneath the sea. As day finally broke, nothing of this once-great ship was visible above the waves. Would the American people ever see the historic *Monitor* again?

FIND OUT MORE

A SUNKEN LEGEND

For more than a century, the *Monitor*'s whereabouts remained a mystery. Then, in 1973, a team of divers from Duke University, North Carolina, discovered the wreck site. A year later, the site became the United States' first National Marine Sanctuary.

On March 9, 1862, the Monitor *fought for four hours with the CSS* Virginia *of the Confederate fleet at the Battle of Hampton Roads. This was the first naval battle between two ironclad warships.*

BATTLE BOATS

Specially built for the US Navy in the American Civil War, the *Monitor* was a new kind of warship. Among its most innovative features was a low-lying hull to avoid being damaged by cannon fire and a revolving gun turret equipped with two guns.

Crewmen survey the dented turret after the battle.

The wreck of the Monitor lies on the Atlantic seabed, to the southeast of Cape Hatteras. Since its sinking, it has become an artificial reef, teeming with different fish species.

Numerous small items have been retrieved from the Monitor site.

RESCUE MISSION

Since the *Monitor*'s discovery, many artifacts, including the anchor, propeller, and gun turret, together with personal belongings of the crew, have been raised from the wreck. The race is now on to preserve the iron hull itself, which is decaying fast in the seawater.

The Monitor's famous revolving gun turret was brought to the surface in 2002.

One of Monitor's guns is placed in a protective bath.

DE LA SALLE'S LOST SHIP

"That's it—I believe this trip is truly cursed."

As he watched his rapidly sinking ship, *La Belle*, Pierre Tessier began to count the cost of his ill-fated mission. Of a crew of 27, only a handful had survived the storm that had blown *La Belle* out of control onto a sandbar. The survivors were stranded on a desolate stretch of coast, plagued by mosquitoes and deadly snakes. The only way back home lay across hostile Indian territory.

La Belle was one of four ships on an expedition to North America led by French nobleman Robert de La Salle. Having made his fortune in the fur trade, he now had the king's blessing to establish a French colony at the mouth of the Mississippi River. The ships reached the Gulf of Mexico in November 1684 but failed to find the delta. They landed at Matagorda Bay in Texas, 405 miles (650 kilometers) off course.

Having established a fort on the coast, de La Salle set off on foot to explore farther afield, leaving the ship in Tessier's command, 30 miles (48 km) from the fort. With no sign of de La Salle, Tessier took the fateful decision to return to the fort. The storm that had blown *La Belle* aground left it just a quarter of a mile (400 meters) off the shore. For a few days, the survivors salvaged as much as they could. But *La Belle* was already sinking, and for three centuries it lay buried in the bay.

FIND OUT MORE

TIME TREASURES

La Belle sank in 1686 but was rediscovered in 1995 by a team of archaeologists from Texas. Using copies of original maps, a survey was made of Matagorda Bay and divers were sent down to investigate.

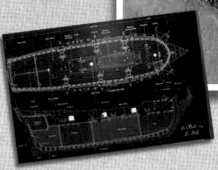

A modern blueprint of La Belle

A cofferdam was built around the wreck. It allowed water to be replaced by air, creating a dry environment to work in.

In this painting, La Belle is on the left.

LA BELLE RETURNS

Over the next year, the divers recovered over a million artifacts from *La Belle*. From them, archaeologists gained a great deal of valuable information about the past. Finds included a wide variety of weapons—bronze cannon, muskets, and shot—and thousands of beads, bells, combs, and pins intended for trade. The ship itself was taken apart timber by timber and removed from the water.

Bronze cannon from La Belle

French explorer Robert de La Salle claimed the entire Mississippi River Basin for France before exploring the Gulf of Mexico.

After 300 years, the timbers of La Belle are well preserved. The rust-colored patch is where the bronze cannon lay.

All that's left of most ancient shipwrecks is their cargo.

SALVAGING THE PAST

Many other shipwrecks are of significant historical importance, especially those from ancient times. The oldest shipwreck, the *Dokos* in Southern Greece, dates from 2,700 BCE. However, one of the most remarkable ancient objects was found in a wreck off the Greek island of Antikythera.

The Antikythera Mechanism is the relic of a bronze "calendar" clock. A forerunner to the analogue computer, it was built in the first century BCE.

A model of the Uluburun vessel—a Late Bronze Age wreck of a merchant ship in Turkey.

Other treasures from Antikythera include this bronze philosopher's head.

The Uluburun find yielded raw materials like glass and metal ingots, which would have been used to make jewelry.

TREASURE OF THE ATOCHA

"It's no good, Captain, we can't get her hatches open!"

The diver, a local man, gasped for breath as he gave his report to the captain of the waiting boat. He was more used to diving for pearls in the waters around the Caribbean islands than searching for the booty from a treasure ship.

Like the rest of his team, his instructions had been simple—to dive down to the wreck of the Spanish galleon and salvage as much of its treasure as possible. Along with six other ships, it had been caught up in a storm and wrecked a few days earlier off the Florida Keys, sinking under the weight of its valuable cargo. But the Spanish officials who had ordered the search were going to be disappointed: the hatches and portholes of the ship's cargo hold were locked. All they could rescue were two bronze cannons because another storm was on its way, and the rescue boat was forced back to the harbor. The second storm scattered the remains of the ship, so that when the divers returned, all signs of the wreckage were gone.

A few weeks earlier, *Nuestra Señora de Atocha* (Our Lady of Atocha) had loaded up with hundreds of gold and silver ingots, thousands of silver coins, and large numbers of uncut emeralds at the Spanish ports of Cartagena in Colombia and Portobelo in Panama. The ship was also carrying valuable jewelry, tobacco, rosewood, indigo, and copper.

After a series of delays, the fleet left Havana, Cuba, for Spain on September 4, 1622. It was six weeks behind schedule and sailing straight into the hurricane season. Within two days, a violent storm drove the fleet onto the treacherous coral reefs off the Florida Keys. With its hull badly damaged, the *Atocha*, and all its treasure, sank quickly. Only five of *Atocha*'s crew—three sailors and two slaves—were rescued. Despite the best efforts of the Spanish, the ship and its fabulous treasure seemed destined to lie forgotten on the bed of the sea.

FIND OUT MORE

BOOTY SHIPS

Then, in the 1960s, American treasure hunter Mel Fisher began his search for the *Atocha*. After 16 years, his team finally located the wreck site in July 1985. The wreckage was scattered for many miles across the sea floor.

A solid gold bullion from the Atocha

The haul from the Atocha included everyday items that would have been used by the crew, like this silver fork, spoon, and dish.

Mel Fisher's salvage boat Dauntless *works off the Atocha wreck site.*

A 1720 map shows the routes of Spanish treasure fleets.

RICH PLUNDER

In today's money, the *Atocha's* cargo is valued at hundreds of millions of dollars. Among the extraordinary treasures found by Fisher's team were gold and silver coins, gold chains, a jewel-encrusted belt, and an emerald and gold cross and ring.

THE TREASURE TRADE

The *Atocha* was one of 28 ships that made up the Spanish treasure fleet. Each year, the fleet sailed from Spain to the Caribbean, carrying provisions for the Spanish colonies in Central and South America. On the return journey, vast riches made up their cargo.

Urca de Lima was another Spanish galleon wrecked off Florida. Part of a treasure convoy hit by a hurricane in 1715, Urca de Lima has yielded rare golden coins, silver cob coins, and other riches.

A diver inspects the wreck site of the Urca de Lima.

Sturdy and sleek, Spanish galleons were advanced ships for the times.

RMS *LUSITANIA*

"She's sinking fast. Let's down periscope and run for home."

As Kapitanleutnant Schweiger spoke, he watched the stricken British liner tilt to starboard and begin to sink beneath the waves. His job here done, there was still the risk of his German U-20 submarine being rammed or fired on. It was time to head for home.

It was early afternoon on May 7, 1915. Britain and Germany had been at war for nine months. The liner, RMS *Lusitania*, was on its way from New York to Liverpool with almost 2,000 passengers and crew on board.

Passengers had been warned that the Atlantic Ocean was now a war zone. That meant that any ship flying a British flag was in danger of being destroyed by German submarines. However, none of those on board truly believed that Germany would carry out its threat and attack an unarmed passenger steamer.

On May 7, the *Lusitania* was around 30 miles (50 kilometers) off the south coast of Ireland, where it encountered fog and reduced its speed. With only a few hours to go until it reached its home port, it crossed right in front of the U-20.

The torpedo struck the *Lusitania* under its bridge, sending a plume of water, metal, and debris into the air. Then, a few minutes later, an even bigger explosion ripped the liner's starboard bow apart. The ship's captain sent out an SOS and gave the order to abandon ship. Immediately the ship began to tilt badly, giving the passengers little chance to escape. Just 18 minutes after being hit, the *Lusitania* sank beneath the waves.

Of the 1,959 people on board, some 1,198 were killed, but a huge controversy over their deaths was only just beginning.

FIND OUT MORE

A VILLAINOUS ACT?

Built in 1907, RMS *Lusitania* was one of the biggest, fastest, and safest liners. Its sinking caused an uproar both in Britain and in the United States and may have contributed to the United States' decision to join the war against Germany in 1917.

THE CONTROVERSY

Because of the second explosion, some people believed that the submarine must have fired a second torpedo, even though Captain Schweiger always denied the claim. Others thought that the *Lusitania* must have been carrying a secret cargo of high explosives for the war effort.

The outrage quickly became used for Allied war propaganda.

IRISHMEN AVENGE THE LUSITANIA

JOIN AN IRISH REGIMENT TO-DAY.

Later investigations found that the Lusitania was only carrying small arms ammunition, which could not have caused the second explosion.

TAKE UP THE SWORD OF JUSTICE

A poster implores the British public to avenge the innocent victims of the sinking.

A replica of a medal struck in Germany, which showed a heavily-armed Lusitania sinking.

When Fr[...]ly began to admire You, my friend, was when you pulled that Lusitania job. When You did that, I said to myself— 'There's a man after my own heart!'"

BARRON COLLIER *Patriotic Series* N⁰ 2

A US poster shows a devil seated with his arm around the shoulders of Kaiser Wilhelm II.

THE INFLUENCE

Of the 139 US citizens aboard the *Lusitania*, 128 lost their lives. However, American leaders refused to overreact. While the American public was not ready for war in 1915, the path to an eventual declaration of war had been set.

The American millionaire Alfred Gwynne Vanderbilt was seen helping children into lifeboats before he died.

President Wilson announced the break in official relations with Germany on February 3, 1917.

The Lusitania was still a potent symbol when it came time for US civilians to join the Great War.

In 1935, divers using armored diving suits located and explored the wreck of the Lusitania for the first time.

Watches from the Lusitania

THE WRECK

In 1993, Robert Ballard, discoverer of the *Titanic*, made a thorough investigation of the wreck of the *Lusitania*. He argued that the second explosion was caused by exploding coal dust. Others believe an explosion in the ship's steam-generating room was much more likely.

One of Lusitania's propellers

ENIGMA OF THE *U-110*
"Now this is a prize even Blackbeard would have been proud of!"

As the Royal Navy destroyer HMS *Bulldog* drew alongside the wounded German submarine, Captain Baker-Cresswell knew that the prize he had been waiting for was finally within his grasp. It was May 9, 1941. Commanded by Kapitanleutnant Lemp, the *U-110* had already been badly damaged in an earlier depth charge. As its crew scrambled desperately onto the decks, HMS *Bulldog* and *Broadway* were waiting to open fire.

But instead of using their deck gun, the crew of the *U-110* had been given the order to abandon ship. Seeing the German sailors trying to leave the ship, the British gave the order to cease fire. *Bulldog* and *Broadway* closed in to capture the U-boat and stop it from sinking. Like his crew, Lemp, too, believed the boat was sinking and abandoned ship. When he realized it was still afloat, he desperately tried to swim back again to make sure the British didn't seize the *U-110*'s secret cargo.

Lemp did not make it back to the *U-110* and would never be seen again. Instead, the *Bulldog*'s crew boarded the boat and stripped it of everything they could carry. Among the items they found was the cargo that Lemp was so desperate to keep from them—top secret German codebooks and an Enigma machine. But the sailors had to be very careful. The codebooks had been printed in ink that would dissolve if the books were dropped in seawater.

Anxious to ensure that the Germans knew nothing about the *U-110*'s capture and would not change their codes, the navy named the mission Operation Primrose, and every sailor was sworn to secrecy. It would remain one of the biggest secrets of World War II. Meanwhile, the *U-110* itself was towed back to Britain and "accidentally" sank on the way home. For the time being, its secret was going to be safe.

FIND OUT MORE

DIVE! DIVE! DIVE!

The captured documents helped British codebreakers at Bletchley Park in England crack a top-secret, handwritten German code used when there was no Enigma machine available.

An Enigma machine (left) was a German machine used to send top-secret codes.

U-BOAT WRECKS

The wrecks of many World War II submarines litter the ocean floor. Though many are war graves, some have been raised and recovered. The German *U-534* (below) was sunk by a British aircraft on May 5, 1945. In 1993, a Danish millionaire paid for it to be raised, hoping to find gold and other treasure on board.

U-110 *is one of many World War II U-boats slowly rotting on the Atlantic seabed.*

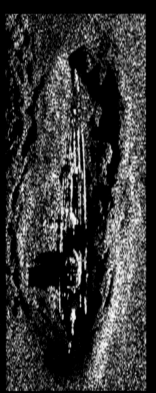

A sonar picture of the wreck of U-166—a 5,000-foot (1,500 meter) deep grave for 52 German sailors in the Gulf of Mexico.

When the U-534 (below) was raised to the surface, there was no gold or treasure to be found. Today, the submarine is on display in the U-Boat Story exhibition at Woodside, Merseyside, UK.

A U-boat is destroyed by a US Navy depth charge during World War II.

LOST TO THE DEPTHS

More recently, the wrecking of several modern submarines has made the headlines. The *Kursk*, a Russian nuclear submarine, sank in the Barents Sea on August 12, 2000, with the loss of its entire crew. It is thought that one of the *Kursk*'s torpcdoes exploded.

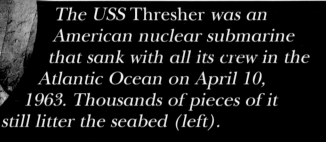

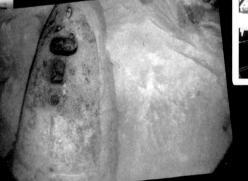

The USS Thresher *was an American nuclear submarine that sank with all its crew in the Atlantic Ocean on April 10, 1963. Thousands of pieces of it still litter the seabed (left).*

The nuclear sub USS Scorpion *(left) was declared lost on June 5, 1968, in the Atlantic.*

The bow section of the sunken USS Scorpion *still contains two nuclear torpedoes. The reason for its sinking remains a mystery.*

In 2000 an intact Civil War era submarine, the Hunley, *was successfully raised from Charleston Harbor.*

The Confederate States ship Hunley *(left) was the first submarine to sink an enemy warship. Launched in 1863, it was sunk itself in 1864 with the loss of its crew.* Hunley *is now being restored (right).*

GLOSSARY

Archaeologist A person who studies the past by looking at ancient places and objects. Marine archaeologists study underwater places.

Artifact A man-made object of archaeological interest from the past.

Ballast Heavy material that is placed in the hold of a ship to make it more stable.

Cofferdam A watertight structure that surrounds an area underwater that is pumped dry so work can be carried out.

Earthworks Man-made banks of earth that used to be built as fortifications to protect a town.

Flagship The most important ship in a fleet; the ship belonging to the commander of the fleet.

Galley A type of ship propelled by sails or oars that was used in ancient and medieval times.

Haven A shelter used as a place of safety.

Ironclad A 19th-century warship made from iron or wood and protected by iron armor plating.

Salvage To save or rescue goods from a ship wrecked at sea.

Scuttled To purposely sink a ship by making openings in the bottom.

Squall A sudden, violent rush of wind, often bringing rain or even snow.

Submersible A small craft that is designed to explore underwater.

Telemotor The control system for the *Titanic*'s steering gear.

Tudor The years between 1485 and 1603 when England was ruled by the Tudor royal family.

FURTHER INFORMATION

ORGANIZATIONS AND WEB SITES

The Battleship *Bismarck*
Web site: http://www.kbismarck.com

Expedition *Whydah*
(508) 487-8899
Web site: http://www.whydah.com

Lusitania Online
Web site: http://www.lusitania.net

The *Mary Rose* Trust
HM Naval Base
Portsmouth PO1 3LX
United Kingdom
+44(0)23 9281 2931
Web site: http://www.maryrose.org

RMS *Titanic*, Inc.
3340 Peachtree Road NE
Suite 2250
Atlanta, GA 30326
(404) 842-2600
Web site: http://www.rmstitanic.net

USS *Monitor* Center
100 Museum Drive
Newport News, VA 23606
(757) 591-7744
Web site:
http://www.marinersmuseum.org/uss-monitor-center/uss-monitor-center

FOR FURTHER READING

Adams, Simon. *Eyewitness: Titanic.* New York, NY: Dorling Kindersley, 2009.

Clifford, Barry. *Real Pirates: The Untold Story of the Whydah from Slave Ship to Pirate Ship.* Washington, DC: National Geographic Society, 2008.

Jeffrey, Gary, and Claudia Saraceni. *Graphic Discoveries: Spectacular Shipwrecks.* New York, NY: Rosen Publishing, 2008.

Porterfield, Jason. *Shipwreck: True Stories of Survival.* New York: Rosen Publishing, 2007.

INDEX

WEB SITES

Due to the changing nature of Internet links, Rosen Publishing has developed an online list of Web sites related to the subject of this book. This site is updated regularly. Please use this link to access this list: http://www.rosenlinks.com/ita/ship